U.S. HISTORY IN REVIEW

THE EMANCIPATION PROCLAMATION

BY KATHRYN WALTON

Enslow PUBLISHING

Please visit our website, www.enslow.com. For a free color catalog of all our high-quality books, call toll free 1-800-398-2504 or fax 1-877-980-4454.

Library of Congress Cataloging-in-Publication Data
Names: Walton, Kathryn, 1993- author.
Title: The Emancipation Proclamation / Kathryn Walton.
Description: Buffalo, New York : Enslow Publishing, [2024] | Series: U.S. history in review | Includes index.
Identifiers: LCCN 2023003408 (print) | LCCN 2023003409 (ebook) | ISBN 9781978536128 (library binding) | ISBN 9781978536111 (paperback) | ISBN 9781978536135 (ebook)
Subjects: LCSH: United States. President (1861-1865 : Lincoln). Emancipation Proclamation–Juvenile literature. | Lincoln, Abraham, 1809-1865–Juvenile literature. | Slaves–Emancipation–United States–Juvenile literature. | United States–Politics and government–1861-1865–Juvenile literature.
Classification: LCC E453 .W24 2024 (print) | LCC E453 (ebook) | DDC 973.7/14–dc23/eng/20230125
LC record available at https://lccn.loc.gov/2023003408
LC ebook record available at https://lccn.loc.gov/2023003409

Published in 2024 by
Enslow Publishing
2544 Clinton Street
Buffalo, NY 14224

Portions of this work were originally authored by Seth Lynch and published as *The Emancipation Proclamation*. All new material this edition authored by Kathryn Walton.

Designer: Leslie Taylor
Editor: Natalie Humphrey

Photo credits: Cover, p. 17 Everett Collection/Shutterstock.com; series art (grunge flag) Andrey Kuzmin/Shutterstock.com; series art (stamp icon) Stocker_team/Shutterstock.com; series art (font) santstock/Shutterstock.com; p. 5 Everett Collection/Shutterstock.com; p. 6 H. C. Howard/https://commons.wikimedia.org/wiki/File:Abraham_Lincoln_presidency_campaign_banner.jpg; p. 7 (dollar bill) Confederate States of America./https://commons.wikimedia.org/wiki/File:Confederate_100_Dollars.jpg, (map) Rainer Lesniewski/Shutterstock.com; p. 9 Everett Collection/Shutterstock.com; p. 11 Morphart Creation/Shutterstock.com; p. 13 Everett Collection/Shutterstock.com; p. 15 Everett Collection/Shutterstock.com; p. 18 Almix/Shutterstock.com; p. 19 Everett Collection/Shutterstock.com; p. 21 Everett Collection/Shutterstock.com; p. 23 Everett Collection/Shutterstock.com; p. 25 Everett Collection/Shutterstock.com; p. 27 Everett Collection/Shutterstock.com; p. 28 AmolRoy/Shutterstock; p. 29 WESTOCK PRODUCTIONS/Shutterstock.com.

Printed in the United States of America

CPSIA compliance information: Batch #CSENS24: For further information, contact Enslow Publishing at 1-800-398-2504.

Contents

War on the Way....4
President Abraham Lincoln....6
Congress Makes a Stand....10
The First Emancipation Proclamation....14
The Final Proclamation....16
No More Fighting....20
U.S. Soldiers....22
Slavery in Border States....24
The Thirteenth Amendment....26
Juneteenth....28
Timeline....30
Glossary....31
For More Information....32
Index....32

*Words in the glossary appear in **bold** the first time they are used in the text.*

War on the Way

When some states joined the United States in the later 1800s, they could choose if they wanted to allow **slavery**. By this time, most Northern states didn't allow slavery. Southern states did. Slavery was important to the Southern economy, or how money was made there.

Learn More

At this time, members of the Republican **political party** mostly wanted to keep slavery from spreading. Leaders of a group of Southern states said they would secede, or break away, if someone from the Republican Party won the presidency in 1860.

Abraham Lincoln

President Abraham Lincoln

The Republican Party **candidate** in 1860 was Abraham Lincoln. He won the **election** for president. By the time he took office on March 4, 1861, seven states had seceded. This would rise to 11 states total. These states came together to form the Confederate States of America.

Learn More

On April 12, 1861, the American Civil War began. Confederate soldiers fired on U.S. troops at Fort Sumter in Charleston, South Carolina.

Lincoln's inaugural address, 1861

President Lincoln didn't work to end slavery right away. He wanted to keep the nation together. He wanted to bring the seceded states back into the United States. Lincoln said he wouldn't end slavery in states that didn't try to leave the United States.

map showing Union, border, and Confederate states

Learn More

Missouri, Kentucky, Maryland, Delaware, and West Virginia were states that allowed slavery that didn't want to secede. These states were called border states. Lincoln didn't want to lose these states by banning slavery.

Congress Makes a Stand

In August 1861, Congress acted against the **rebellion**. It passed the first Confiscation Act. This act said the United States could confiscate, or take, anything that belonged to the Confederates. However, because the Confederacy didn't consider itself part of the United States, this act was hard to **enforce**.

Learn More

The first Confiscation Act also said that enslaved people working or fighting for the Confederate army were free. In 1862, Congress passed a second Confiscation Act that said people enslaved by Confederate officials in some areas were free.

Here, enslaved people who were fighting for the Confederate army are freed by the Confiscation Act of 1861.

When Congress passed the second Confiscation Act, Lincoln felt he had enough support, or help, to act. He wrote the **preliminary** Emancipation Proclamation in July 1862. This **document** was issued, or put forth, on September 22, 1862.

Learn More

After hearing the preliminary proclamation, some members of Lincoln's **cabinet** were worried. They believed the proclamation went too far.

The First Emancipation Proclamation

The preliminary proclamation was a **warning** for the Confederate states. Lincoln gave them 100 days to stop rebelling. He wrote that if they didn't, all enslaved people in the Confederate states still fighting would be set free. Even with Lincoln's warning, the Civil War continued.

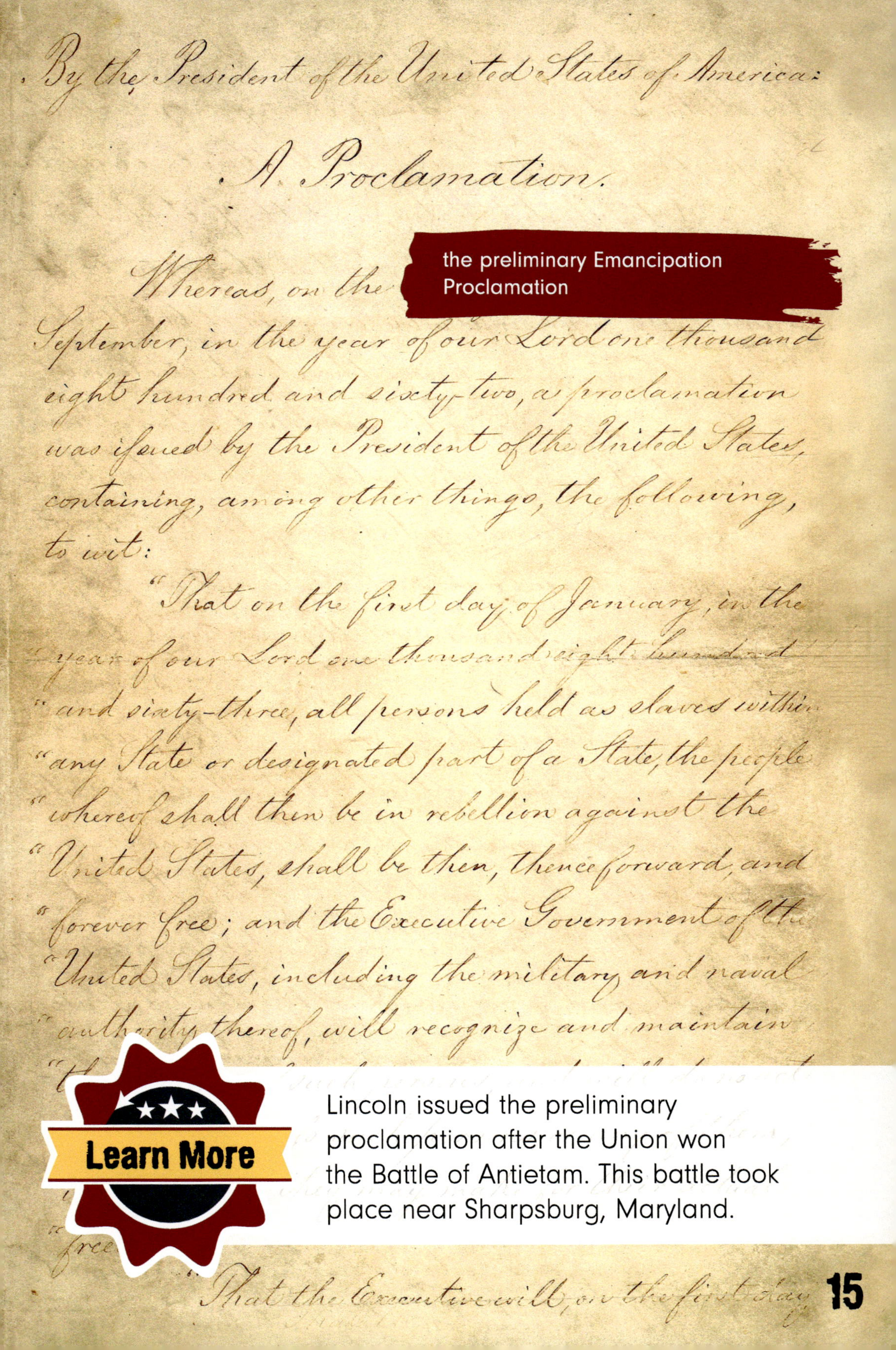
By the President of the United States of America:

A Proclamation.

Whereas, on the

September, in the year of our Lord one thousand eight hundred and sixty-two, a proclamation was issued by the President of the United States, containing, among other things, the following, to wit:

"That on the first day of January, in the year of our Lord one thousand eight hundred "and sixty-three, all persons held as slaves within "any State or designated part of a State, the people "whereof shall then be in rebellion against the "United States, shall be then, thenceforward, and "forever free; and the Executive Government of the "United States, including the military and naval "authority thereof, will recognize and maintain

"free

"That the Executive will, on the first day

the preliminary Emancipation Proclamation

Learn More

Lincoln issued the preliminary proclamation after the Union won the Battle of Antietam. This battle took place near Sharpsburg, Maryland.

The Final Proclamation

On January 1, 1863, Lincoln issued the final, or last, Emancipation Proclamation. Lincoln didn't call a cabinet meeting when he signed the proclamation. Only a few of Lincoln's friends were with him when he signed the document at the White House.

Learn More

Before he signed the Emancipation Proclamation, Lincoln said, "I never, in my life, felt more certain that I was doing right than I do in signing this paper."

The Emancipation Proclamation stated that as of January 1, 1863, all enslaved people living in the Confederate states still fighting would be "forever free." The U.S. government would support this freedom, and no part of the government would stop enslaved people from becoming and staying free.

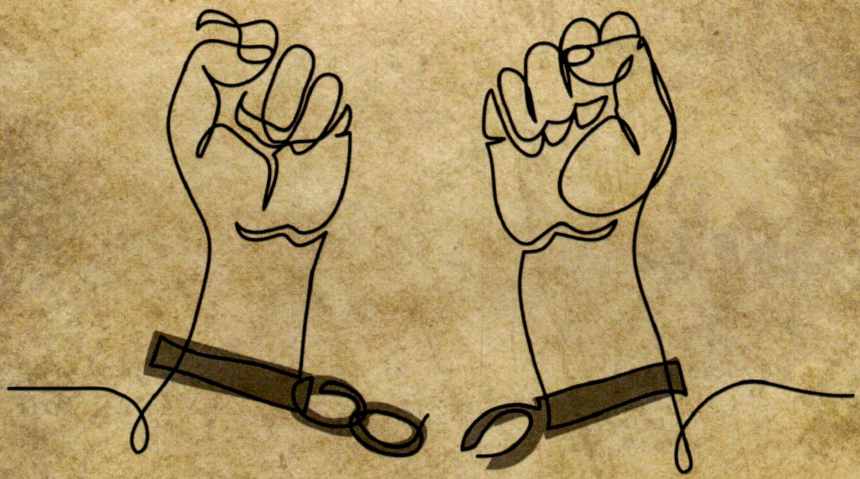

Learn More

Even though the Emancipation Proclamation would free many enslaved people, some people believed it didn't go far enough.

No More Fighting

In the Emancipation Proclamation, Lincoln also asks freedmen, or enslaved people that were now free, not to fight unless they had to. Since there was already a war going on, Lincoln may have wanted to stop more fighting.

Learn More

Lincoln also said freedmen should work for money wherever they could.

U.S. Soldiers

Even though freedmen were asked not to fight on their own, Lincoln welcomed them into the Union army if they wanted. This was an important addition. As the fighting went on, both the Union and Confederate armies needed more men to fight.

Company E, 4th U.S. Colored Infantry

Learn More

Nearly 200,000 Black men fought for the Union army by the end of the war.

Slavery in Border States

The Emancipation Proclamation only ended slavery in Confederate states that were still fighting. It didn't end slavery in border states. Parts of Louisiana and the part of Virginia that would become West Virginia were written **exceptions** to the proclamation.

Freedmen were hired to work as helpers to these Union officers.

Learn More

Lincoln believed Congress would need to pass a law to end slavery. He didn't believe he had the power to do it.

The Thirteenth Amendment

The Emancipation Proclamation didn't end slavery across the United States, but it was a step in the right direction. After the war finally ended in 1865, Congress approved the Thirteenth **Amendment**. It abolished, or banned, slavery in the United States.

Learn More

On April 14, 1865, an actor named John Wilkes Booth shot President Lincoln. Lincoln died the next day. He wouldn't see the official end of the Civil War in April 1865.

Juneteenth

Not every once-enslaved person knew slavery was over. Some enslavers didn't tell those they had enslaved about this until much later. In Texas, these people didn't learn they were free until June 19, 1865. This day is now a holiday called Juneteenth.

Learn More

Texas made Juneteenth a state holiday in 1980. Juneteenth became a federal, or national, holiday in 2021.

Timeline

November 1860
Abraham Lincoln is elected the 16th president of the United States.

December 20, 1860
South Carolina is the first state to secede.

March 4, 1861
Lincoln takes office as president.

April 12, 1861
The American Civil War starts after shots are fired at Fort Sumter.

August 6, 1861
Congress passes the First Confiscation Act.

July 17, 1862
Congress passes the Second Confiscation Act.

September 22, 1862
Lincoln issues the preliminary Emancipation Proclamation.

January 1, 1863
Lincoln issues the full Emancipation Proclamation.

April 9, 1865
The Civil War ends.

December 6, 1865
The Thirteenth Amendment ends slavery.

Glossary

amendment: A change or addition to a constitution.

cabinet: A group of senior officials appointed by the president as special advisors.

candidate: A person running for a government position.

document: A formal piece of writing.

election: The act of voting someone into a government position.

enforce: To make sure people obey the law.

exception: A case in which a rule or law does not apply.

political party: A group of people with similar beliefs about how the government should be run.

preliminary: Something that comes before a main document or work.

rebellion: The act of fighting to overthrow a government.

slavery: The state of being owned by another person and forced to work without pay.

warning: Letting others know something may happen.

For More Information

Books

Kerry, Isaac. *The Attack on Fort Sumter: A Day That Changed America*. North Mankato, MN: Capstone Press, 2023.

Silva, Sadie. *The Civil War*. Buffalo, NY: Enslow Publishing, 2023.

Website

DK Findout!
www.dkfindout.com/us/history/american-civil-war/emancipation-proclamation/
Learn more about the Emancipation Proclamation and the Civil War.

Publisher's note to educators and parents: *Our editors have carefully reviewed this website to ensure that it is suitable for students. Many websites change frequently, however, and we cannot guarantee that a site's future contents will continue to meet our high standards of quality and educational value. Be advised that students should be closely supervised whenever they access the internet.*

Index

border states, 9, 24

Civil War, 7, 14, 26, 27, 30

Confederate States of America, 6, 9, 10, 11, 12, 14, 18, 24

Confiscation Acts, 10, 11, 30

Emancipation Proclamation, 16, 17, 18, 19, 20, 24, 26, 30

freedmen, 20, 21, 22, 25

Juneteenth, 28, 29

Lincoln, Abraham, 6, 8, 9, 12, 14, 15, 16, 17, 20, 21, 22, 25, 27, 30

preliminary Emancipation Proclamation, 12, 13, 14, 15, 30

secede, 5, 6, 30

slavery, 4, 5, 8, 9, 25, 26, 28, 30

Thirteenth Amendment, 26, 30